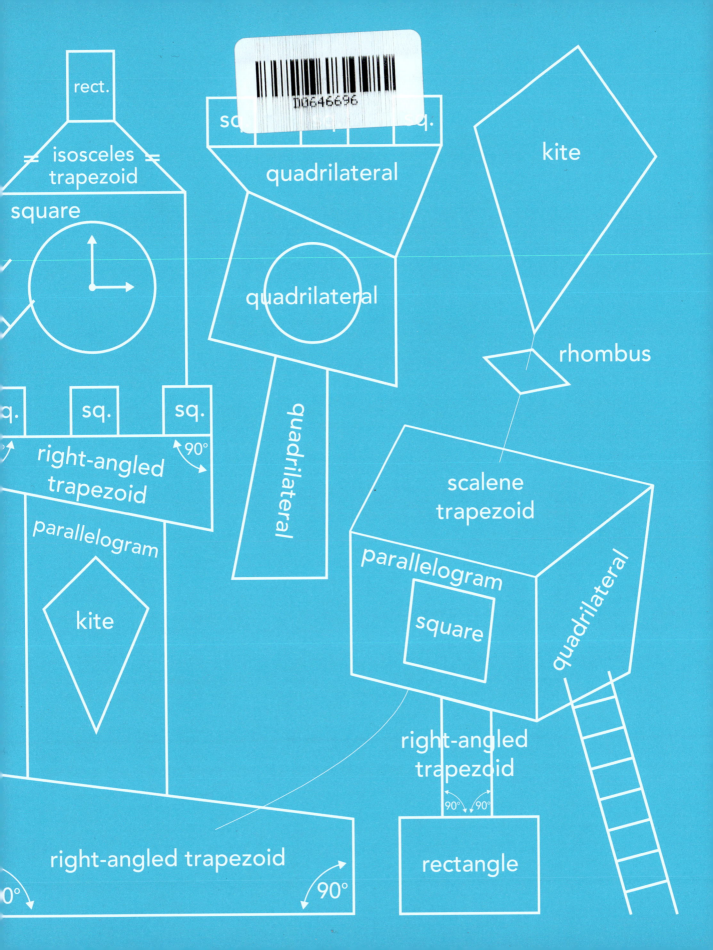

rect.

isosceles
trapezoid

square

sc... ...q.

quadrilateral

kite

quadrilateral

rhombus

sq. sq. sq.

90°

right-angled
trapezoid

parallelogram

kite

quadrilateral

scalene
trapezoid

parallelogram

square

right-angled
trapezoid

90° 90°

right-angled trapezoid

rectangle

quadrilateral

0°

90°

SQUARES, RECTANGLES, and other QUADRILATERALS

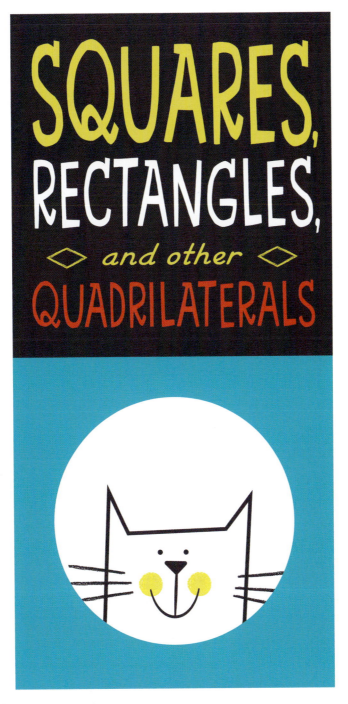

by David A. Adler

illustrated by Edward Miller

Holiday House  New York

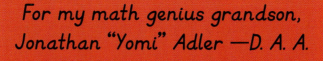

For my math genius grandson,
Jonathan "Yomi" Adler —D. A. A.

To my mother —E. M.

Text copyright © 2018 by David A. Adler
Illustrations copyright © 2018 by Edward Miller
All Rights Reserved
HOLIDAY HOUSE is registered in the U.S. Patent and Trademark Office.
Printed and Bound in August 2018 at Tien Wah Press, Johor Bahu, Johor, Malaysia.
www.holidayhouse.com
First Edition
1 3 5 7 9 10 8 6 4 2

Library of Congress Cataloging-in-Publication Data

Names: Adler, David A. | Miller, Edward, 1964- illustrator.
Title: Squares, rectangles, and other quadrilaterals / by David A. Adler ;
illustrated by Edward Miller.
Description: New York : Holiday House, [2018] | Audience: Age 6-10. |
Audience: K to grade 3.
Identifiers: LCCN 2017010161 | ISBN 9780823437597 (hardcover)
Subjects: LCSH: Quadrilaterals—Juvenile literature. | Square—Juvenile
literature. | Rectangles—Juvenile literature. | Geometry, Solid—
Juvenile literature.
Classification: LCC QA482 .A348 2018 | DDC 516/.154—dc23
LC record available at https://lccn.loc.gov/2017010161

Visit www.davidaadler.com for more information on the author, for a list of his books, and to
download teacher's guides and educational materials. You can also learn more about the writing
process, take fun quizzes, and read selected pages from David A. Adler's books.

Visit Edward Miller on Facebook at www.facebook.com/EdwardElementary

Name
this
shape?

You'd be right if you called it a **square.**

You'd also be right if you called it a **quadrilateral.**

A quadrilateral is a **polygon,** a closed **two-dimensional** or flat figure with **four straight sides.**

A square is a quadrilateral. It's a special kind of quadrilateral.

Take a look at these polygons.

Each has just **four straight**

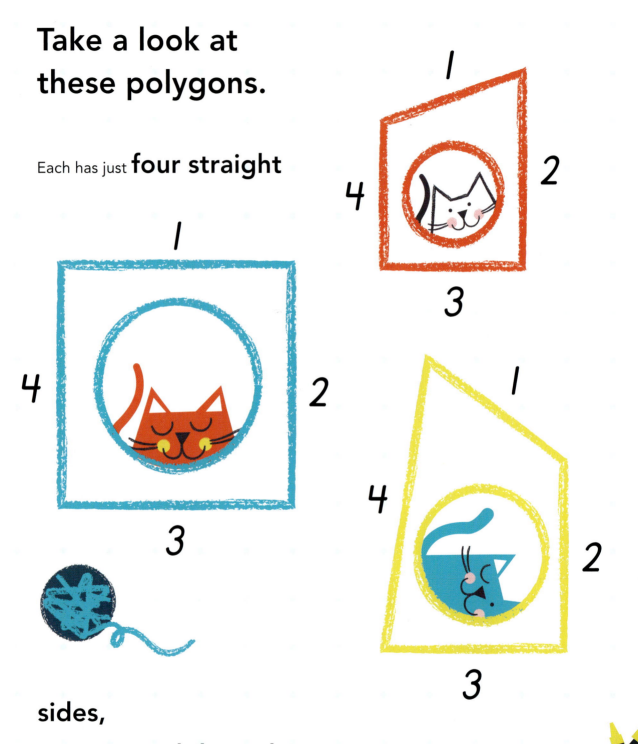

sides,

so each is a **quadrilateral.**

Each quadrilateral also has **four angles,**
located at the points where two sides meet.

The point where the sides meet is called the **vertex** of the angle.

The two straight lines forming each angle are called the **arms** of the angle.

vertex · arm · vertex

1 angle

2 angle

arm

arm

4 angle

angle 3

vertex

arm

5

What makes a square a special kind of quadrilateral?

Use a ruler to measure each side of the square.

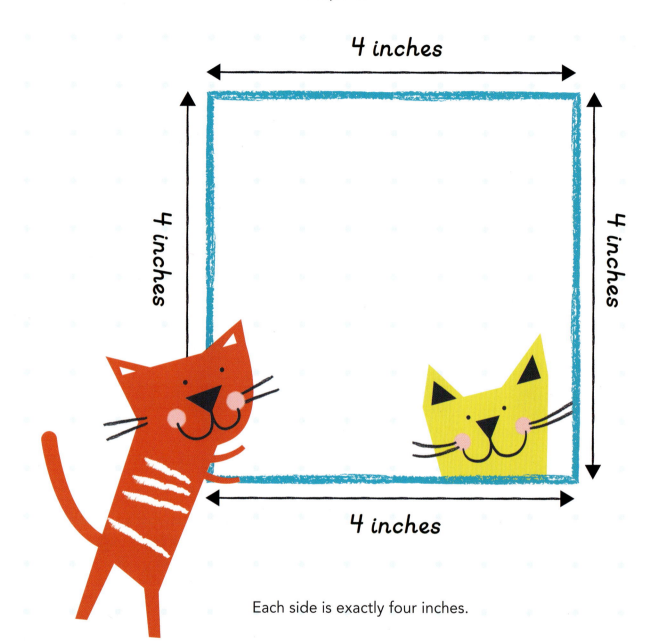

4 inches

4 inches

4 inches

4 inches

Each side is exactly four inches.

All four sides of a square are the same length.

But that's not all.

Look at the square's angles. Each is the same.

Each is a **right angle.**

right
angle

right
angle

right
angle

right
angle

What's a right angle?

One **arm** of a right angle is perfectly horizontal.
The other is perfectly vertical.

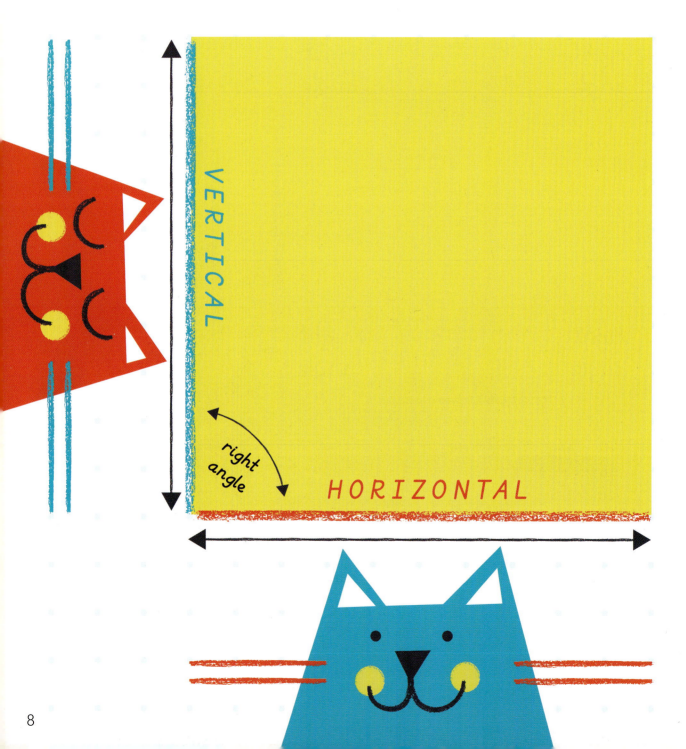

VERTICAL

right angle

HORIZONTAL

You can use an envelope to make a **"right-angle tester."**

Cut off a corner of the envelope, but don't cut it too close to the corner. It should be easy to hold. Now use the envelope corner to check the angles of the square.

Does it exactly fit in each corner of the square? It should. The sides of each corner of the envelope form a right angle.

The outer sides of each corner of a square form a right angle.

You can use an analog clock, a clock with hands, to learn about angles and quadrilaterals.

Think of the hour and minute hands of the clock as arms of an angle. As time passes, the angle changes.

At three o'clock the hands of a clock form a right angle.

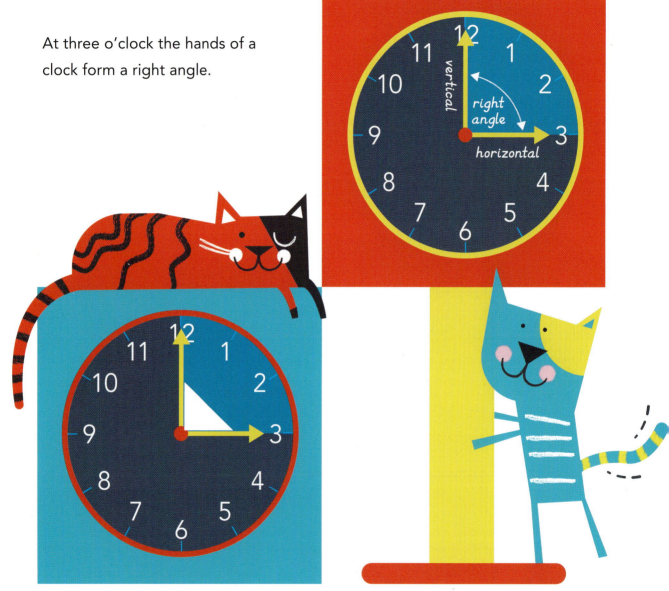

Use your right angle tester, the envelope corner, to check the angle on this clock formed by the hour and minute hands.

It's three o'clock. The angle formed is a right angle.

The size of an angle is measured in degrees. A right angle is 90 degrees.

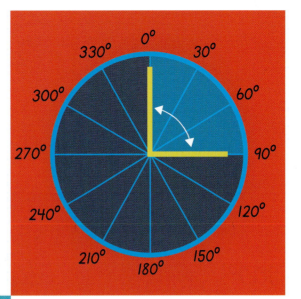

At one o'clock the angle formed by the hands of the clock is smaller than a right angle. The angle formed at one o'clock is 30 degrees.

At four o'clock the angle formed by the hands of the clock is greater than a right angle. The angle formed at four o'clock is 120 degrees.

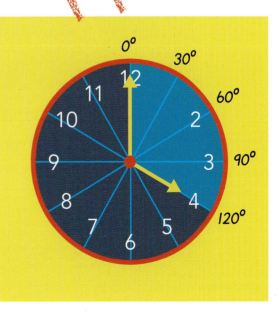

The full measure that the hour hand makes as it travels from noon to midnight, when it circles the clock, is **360 degrees.**

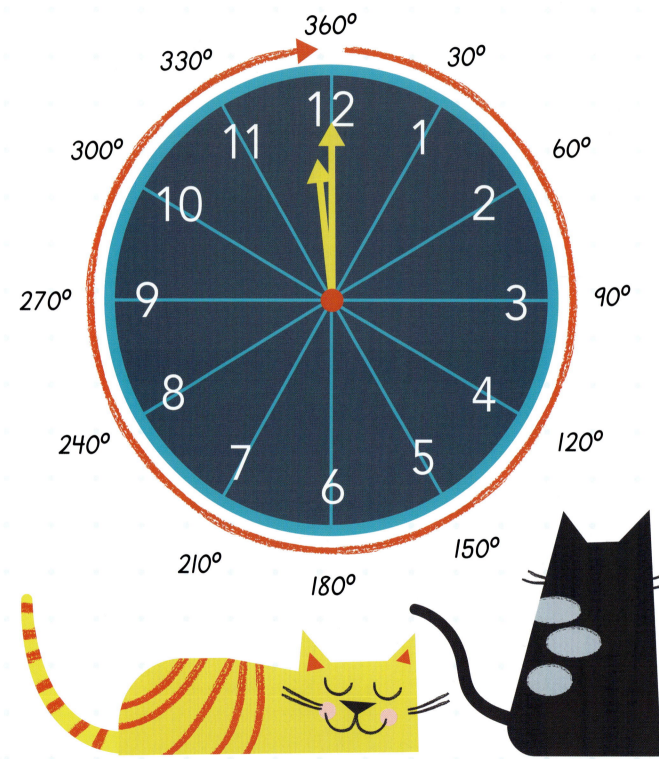

A square has four right angles. Each is 90 degrees.

90°   90°

90°   90°

The total measure of all
four angles of a square

$$
\begin{array}{r}
90° \\
90° \\
90° \\
+\ 90° \\
\hline
=\ 360°
\end{array}
$$

It's the same with
every quadrilateral.
The total measure
of all four angles of
any quadrilateral is
360 degrees.

Prove the total measure of all four angles of a quadrilateral always adds up to 360 degrees.

You'll need

- a pencil
- a colored pencil
- a ruler
- thick paper
- scissors that are safe for you to use

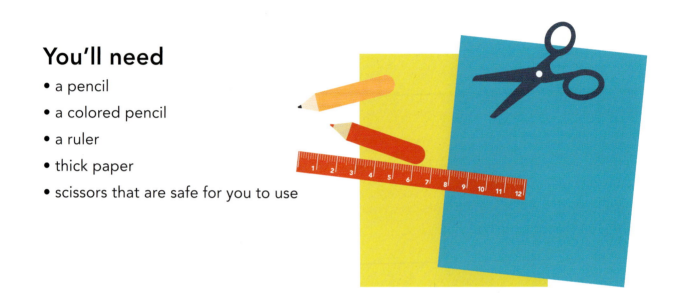

1. With the ruler as a guide, draw two large quadrilaterals. Make one a square and the other oddly shaped.

2. Look at the four angles of your quadrilaterals. Use your right angle tester to measure the angles. Each of the angles of the square will be a right angle. Probably none of the angles of the oddly shaped quadrilateral will be a right angle. Some will be larger and some smaller.

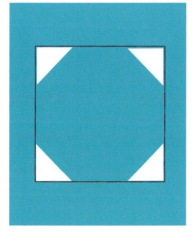

3. Use the colored pencil to mark the vertex of each angle of the quadrilaterals. About an inch away from each vertex draw a curved line from one arm of the angle to the other.

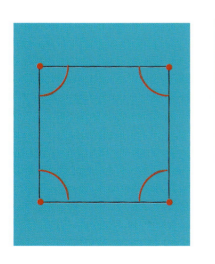

4. You'll need an adult to help or supervise
this next step. Use scissors to cut out
each of the four angles of the square.

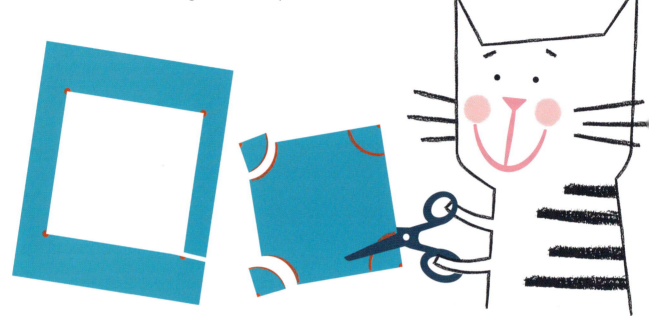

Fit the four angles of the square together,
vertex to vertex. They should fit together
and form an approximate circle.

The total measure of the four angles of a square is 360 degrees.

But we already knew that.

What is the total measure of the four angles of the oddly shaped quadrilateral?

5. Use the scissors to cut out each of the four angles of the oddly shaped quadrilateral.

6. Fit the four angles together, vertex to vertex. They should fit together and form an approximate circle.

The total measure of the four angles of every quadrilateral is 360 degrees.

You can show this another way.

Draw all sorts of angles, some with the arms close together, some with the arms far apart. Let the arms of each angle be two sides of a quadrilateral.

$$140°$$
$$75°$$
$$75°$$
$$+ 70°$$
$$= 360°$$

$$120°$$
$$90°$$
$$90°$$
$$+ 60°$$
$$= 360°$$

90°
120°
90°
60°

70°
140°
75°
75°

If the angle you start with is much larger than a right angle, the angles formed by the additional two sides of the quadrilateral will be smaller.

If the angle you start with is much smaller than a right angle, the angles formed by the additional two sides of the quadrilateral will be larger.

When you're done drawing your quadrilaterals the sum of the angles of each quadrilateral will always be **360 degrees.**

140°
120°
55°
+ 45°
= 360°

130°
90°
70°
+ 70°
= 360°

A square is not the only special kind of quadrilateral.

Take a look at these shapes.

It's a closed figure with just

four straight sides.

It's a quadrilateral—
a special kind of quadrilateral called a

rectangle.

What makes a rectangle a special kind of quadrilateral?

Use a ruler to measure each of its sides.

The base of the rectangle is five inches. The side opposite the base is also five inches.

The two other sides of the rectangle are opposite each other. Each side is two inches.

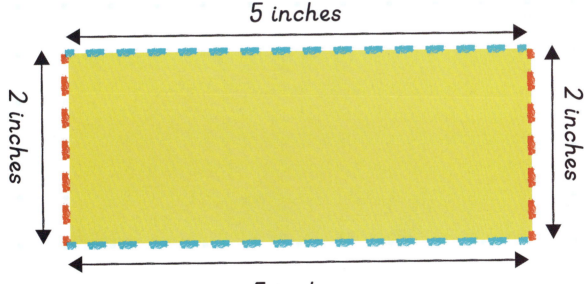

The opposite sides of a rectangle are of equal length.

Now use the envelope corner to check the angles of the rectangle. Does it exactly fit in each corner of the rectangle? It should. Each of a rectangle's four angles is a **right angle.**

The opposite sides of a square are equal. Each of a square's four angles are right angles. A square is a special kind of rectangle because beyond having all the properties of a rectangle it has one more. All of its sides are of **equal** length.

90°   5 inches   90°

5 inches   5 inches

90°   5 inches   90°

Make a new kind of rectangle— a parallelogram.

You will need

- an empty cereal or cracker box
- three crayons or pencils
- your right-angle tester

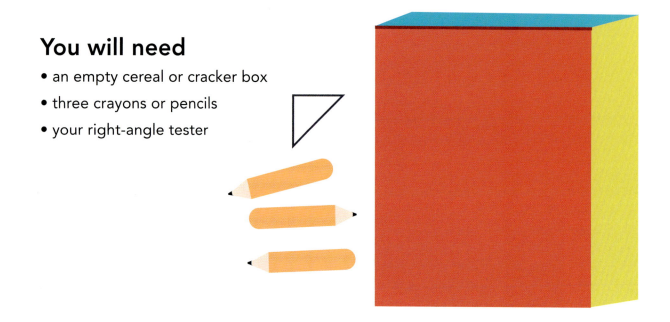

1. Find an empty cereal or cracker box. Cut off the top and bottom flaps. Now look at the box.

Look at the shapes of the four cardboard panels. Each is a rectangle.

2. Rest what's left of the box on a table with one of the two large panels resting directly on the table.

3. Bend down so you are eye level with the box. Look at the open shape made by the edges of the four panels.

4. The edges of the panels should form a shape with four sides and four angles. The sides opposite each other should be the same length.

Use your "right angle tester" on each of the four angles. Each should be a right angle. The edges of the panels should form a rectangle.

5. Now, place two or three crayons or pencils on the top panel of the box. Bend down again so you are eye level with the box. Look at the open shape made by the edges of the four panels. The sides are still the same length. The sides opposite each other are still equal. But look what happened to the angles.

6. Use your "right-angle tester" on each of the four angles. None of the angles is a right angle. Two of the angles are larger and two are smaller. The two larger angles are opposite each other. The two smaller angles are opposite each other.

The shape formed by the edges of the panels is, of course, a quadrilateral, a closed two-dimensional figure with just four straight sides. It's a special kind of quadrilateral. It's a **parallelogram.**

Each pair of opposite sides of a parallelogram are parallel.

That means the sides are always the exact same distance apart. Railroad tracks are parallel. They are always the same distance apart.

3 inches

2 inches

2 inches

3 inches

A rhombus is a special kind of parallelogram.

A parallelogram is a quadrilateral with each pair of opposite sides parallel.

A parallelogram with all four sides the same length is a rhombus.

You may think of a rhombus as a squished square.

4 inches

4 inches

4 inches

4 inches

This quadrilateral has **one pair of parallel sides**. It's not a parallelogram. It's a **trapezoid.**

A trapezoid is a special kind of quadrilateral, and there are special kinds of trapezoids.

A trapezoid with **two nonparallel sides of equal lengths** is an **isosceles trapezoid.**

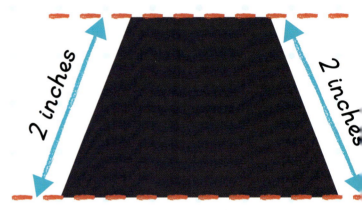

A trapezoid with **two nonparallel sides of different lengths** is a **scalene trapezoid.**

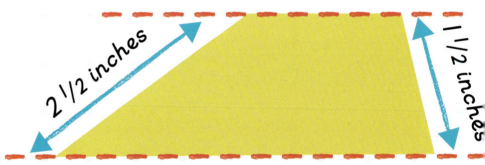

A trapezoid with **two right angles**, one next to the other, is a **right-angled trapezoid.**

This quadrilateral has two pairs of equal sides. Unlike a rectangle or a parallelogram, the sides of equal length are not opposite each other. They are **adjacent,** next to each other. This special kind of quadrilateral looks like a kite, and that's its name, **"kite."**

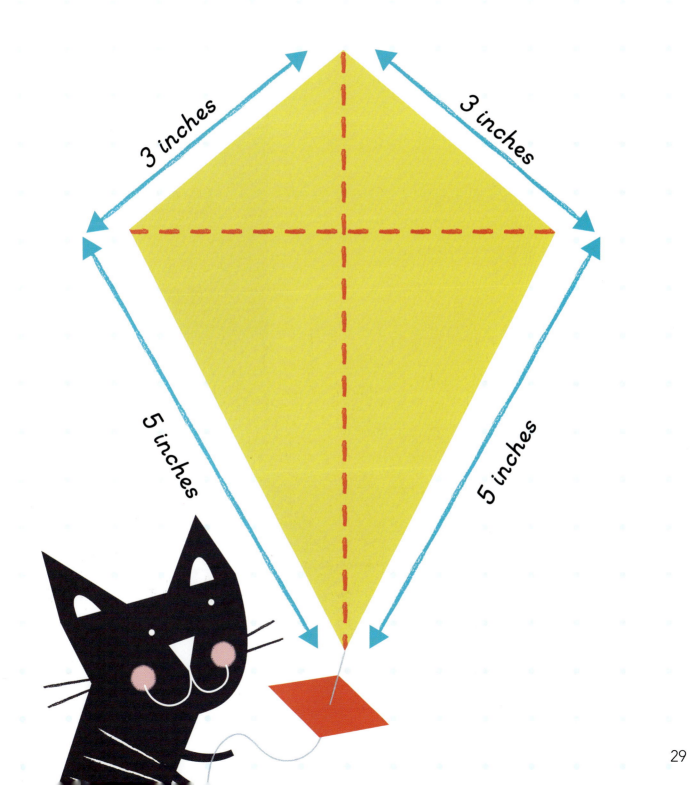

All quadrilaterals are **polygons,** closed two-dimensional (flat) figures with just four straight sides. Some are special kinds of quadrilaterals and some aren't.

How many are squares, rectangles, parallelograms, rhombuses, trapezoids, and kites, and how many aren't?

If they're all closed two-dimensional figures with just four straight sides, they may look very different, but they're all quadrilaterals.

Answers on endpapers

Glossary

angle: the space between two lines that meet. The lines are called the "arms" of the angle, and the size of the angle is measured by the space between the arms, not by the length of the arms.

degree: a unit used to measure angles. There are 360 degrees in a complete circle.

isosceles trapezoid: a quadrilateral that has one pair of sides that are parallel and one pair of sides that are of equal lengths but not parallel. It has two pairs of adjacent matching angles.

parallel lines: lines that are always the same distance apart, like railroad tracks.

parallelogram: a quadrilateral with each pair of opposite sides parallel and of equal length. It has two pairs of opposite matching angles.

polygon: a two-dimensional (flat) shape made up of only straight sides.

quadrilateral: a four-sided polygon.

rectangle: a quadrilateral that has two pairs of opposite sides of equal length and four right angles.

rhombus: a quadrilateral that has four sides of equal length. It has no right angles. It has two pairs of opposite matching angles.

right angle: an angle that is 90 degrees, one quarter of a circle. The corner of an envelope forms a right angle.

scalene trapezoid: a quadrilateral that has one pair of sides that are parallel and one pair of sides that are not parallel. Each of the four sides are of different lengths.

square: a quadrilateral with each of its four side the same length and four right angles.

trapezoid: a quadrilateral that has just one pair of sides that are parallel.

vertex: the point where the two arms of an angle meet.

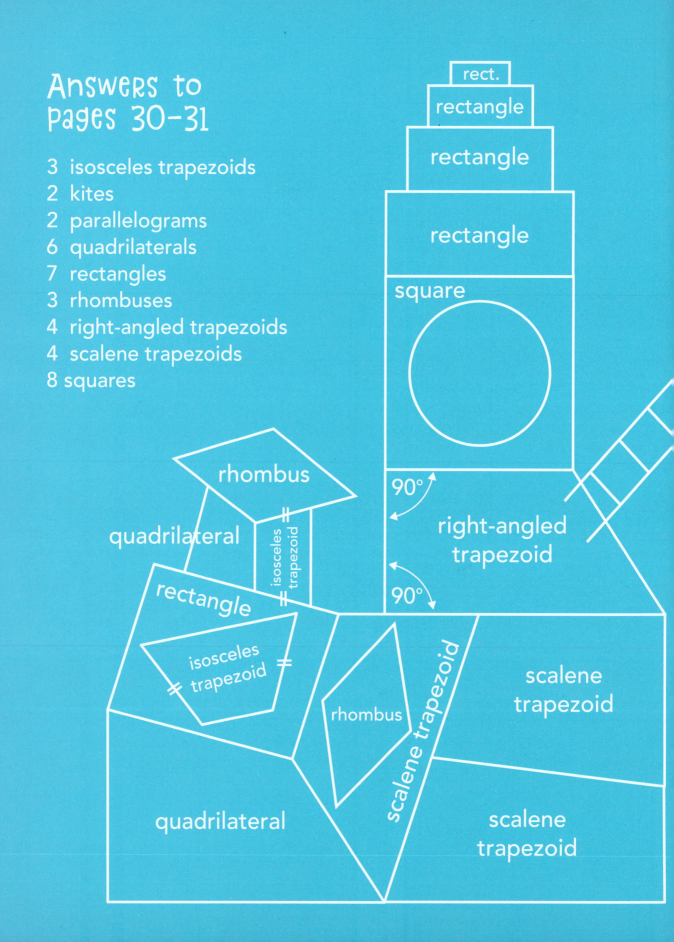

Answers to Pages 30–31

- 3 isosceles trapezoids
- 2 kites
- 2 parallelograms
- 6 quadrilaterals
- 7 rectangles
- 3 rhombuses
- 4 right-angled trapezoids
- 4 scalene trapezoids
- 8 squares

rect.

rectangle

rectangle

rectangle

square

right-angled trapezoid

90°

90°

rhombus

quadrilateral

isosceles trapezoid

rectangle

isosceles trapezoid

rhombus

scalene trapezoid

scalene trapezoid

scalene trapezoid

quadrilateral